To:

Love From:

Measurement Conversion Chart

Imperial	Metric	Cups 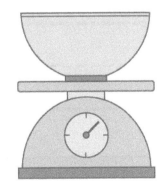
1/2 Fl.oz	15ml	1 Tablespoon
1 Fl.oz	30ml	1/8 Cup
2 Fl.oz	60 ml	1/4 Cup
4 Fl.oz	125ml	1/2 Cup
5 Fl.oz (1/4 pint)	150ml	2/3 Cup
6 Fl.oz	175 ml	3/4 Cup
8 Fl.oz	250 ml	1 Cup
12 Fl.oz	375 ml	1.1/2 Cup
16 Fl.oz	500 ml	2 Cups

Tablespoon	Teaspoon
1	3
2	6
4	12
6	18
8	24
10	30
12	36

Recipe:

Ingredients List:

_____

_____

_____

_____

_____

_____

_____

Prep Time:

_____

Cooking time:

_____

Serves:

_____

Rating:

★★★★★

_____

Equipment List:

_____

_____

_____

_____

_____

_____

_____

Instructions:

Recipe Notes:

Family Holiday Traditions:

_____

_____

_____

_____

_____

_____

_____

Memories to Share:

_____

_____

_____

_____

_____

_____

_____

_____

Notes and Keepsakes:

Recipe:

Ingredients List:

_____

_____

_____

_____

_____

_____

_____

Prep Time:
_____

Cooking time:
_____

Serves:
_____

Rating:
★★★★★

Equipment List:

_____

_____

_____

_____

_____

_____

Instructions:

Recipe Notes:

Family Holiday Traditions:

_____
_____
_____
_____
_____
_____
_____

Memories to Share:

_____
_____
_____
_____
_____
_____
_____
_____

Notes and Keepsakes:

Recipe:

Ingredients List:

_____

_____

_____

_____

_____

_____

Prep Time:

_____

Cooking time:

_____

Serves:

_____

Rating:

★★★★★

_____

Equipment List:

_____

_____

_____

_____

_____

_____

Instructions:

_____

_____

_____

_____

_____

_____

_____

_____

_____

_____

_____

_____

_____

Recipe Notes:

_____

_____

_____

_____

Family Holiday Traditions:

_____

_____

_____

_____

_____

_____

_____

Memories to Share:

_____

_____

_____

_____

_____

_____

_____

_____

Recipe:

Ingredients List:

_____

_____

_____

_____

_____

_____

Prep Time:

_____

Cooking time:

_____

Serves:

_____

Rating:
★★★★★

_____

Equipment List:

_____

_____

_____

_____

_____

_____

_____

Instructions:

_____

_____

_____

_____

_____

_____

_____

_____

_____

_____

_____

_____

_____

Recipe Notes:

_____

_____

_____

_____

Family Holiday Traditions:

Memories to Share:

Recipe:

Ingredients List:

_____

_____

_____

_____

_____

_____

Prep Time:

_____

Cooking time:

_____

Serves:

_____

Rating:

★★★★★

_____

Equipment List:

_____

_____

_____

_____

_____

_____

Instructions:

Recipe Notes:

Family Holiday Traditions:

_____

_____

_____

_____

_____

_____

_____

Memories to Share:

_____

_____

_____

_____

_____

_____

_____

_____

Recipe:

Ingredients List:

_____

_____

_____

_____

_____

_____

_____

Prep Time:

_____

Cooking time:

_____

Serves:

_____

Rating:

★★★★★

Equipment List:

_____

_____

_____

_____

_____

_____

_____

_____

Instructions:

Recipe Notes:

Family Holiday Traditions:

Memories to Share:

Notes and Keepsakes:

Recipe:

Ingredients List:

_____

_____

_____

_____

_____

_____

_____

Prep Time:

_____

Cooking time:

_____

Serves:

_____

Rating:

★★★★★

_____

Equipment List:

_____

_____

_____

_____

_____

_____

_____

Instructions:

Recipe Notes:

Family Holiday Traditions:

Memories to Share:

Notes and Keepsakes:

Recipe:

Ingredients List:

_____

_____

_____

_____

_____

_____

Prep Time:

_____

Cooking time:

_____

Serves:

_____

Rating:

★ ★ ★ ★ ★

_____

Equipment List:

_____

_____

_____

_____

_____

_____

_____

_____

Instructions:

Recipe Notes:

Family Holiday Traditions:

_____

_____

_____

_____

_____

_____

_____

Memories to Share:

_____

_____

_____

_____

_____

_____

_____

_____

Notes and Keepsakes:

Recipe:

Ingredients List:

_____

_____

_____

_____

_____

_____

Prep Time:

_____

Cooking time:

_____

Serves:

_____

Rating:

★★★★★

_____

Equipment List:

_____

_____

_____

_____

_____

_____

_____

_____

Instructions:

_____

_____

_____

_____

_____

_____

_____

_____

_____

_____

_____

Recipe Notes:

_____

_____

_____

Family Holiday Traditions:

Memories to Share:

Notes and Keepsakes:

Recipe:

Ingredients List:

_____

_____

_____

_____

_____

_____

_____

Prep Time:

_____

Cooking time:

_____

Serves:

_____

Rating:

★★★★★

_____

Equipment List:

_____

_____

_____

_____

_____

_____

_____

_____

Instructions:

Recipe Notes:

Family Holiday Traditions:

_____

_____

_____

_____

_____

_____

Memories to Share:

_____

_____

_____

_____

_____

_____

_____

_____

Notes and Keepsakes:

Recipe:

Ingredients List:

_____

_____

_____

_____

_____

_____

Prep Time:

_____

Cooking time:

_____

Serves:

_____

Rating:

★★★★★

_____

Equipment List:

_____

_____

_____

_____

_____

_____

_____

Instructions:

_____

_____

_____

_____

_____

_____

_____

_____

_____

_____

_____

_____

Recipe Notes:

_____

_____

_____

Family Holiday Traditions:

_____

_____

_____

_____

_____

_____

_____

Memories to Share:

_____

_____

_____

_____

_____

_____

_____

Notes and Keepsakes:

Recipe:

Ingredients List:

_____

_____

_____

_____

_____

_____

Prep Time:

_____

Cooking time:

_____

Serves:

_____

Rating:

★★★★★

_____

Equipment List:

_____

_____

_____

_____

_____

_____

_____

_____

Instructions:

_____

_____

_____

_____

_____

_____

_____

_____

_____

_____

_____

Recipe Notes:

_____

_____

_____

Family Holiday Traditions:

Memories to Share:

Notes and Keepsakes:

Recipe:

Ingredients List:

_____

_____

_____

_____

_____

_____

_____

Prep Time:

_____

Cooking time:

_____

Serves:

_____

Rating:

★★★★★

Equipment List:

_____

_____

_____

_____

_____

_____

_____

_____

Instructions:

_____

_____

_____

_____

_____

_____

_____

_____

_____

_____

_____

Recipe Notes:

_____

_____

_____

_____

Family Holiday Traditions:

_____

_____

_____

_____

_____

_____

Memories to Share:

_____

_____

_____

_____

_____

_____

_____

Notes and Keepsakes:

Recipe:

Ingredients List:

Prep Time:

Cooking time:

Serves:

Rating:
★★★★★

Equipment List:

Instructions:

Recipe Notes:

Family Holiday Traditions:

Memories to Share:

Notes and Keepsakes:

Recipe:

Ingredients List:

_____

_____

_____

_____

_____

_____

_____

_____

Prep Time:

_____

Cooking time:

_____

Serves:

_____

Rating:

★★★★★

_____

Equipment List:

_____

_____

_____

_____

_____

_____

_____

_____

Instructions:

Recipe Notes:

Family Holiday Traditions:

Memories to Share:

Notes and Keepsakes:

Recipe:

Ingredients List:

_____

_____

_____

_____

_____

_____

_____

_____

Prep Time:

_____

Cooking time:

_____

Serves:

_____

Rating:

★★★★★

_____

Equipment List:

_____

_____

_____

_____

_____

_____

_____

_____

Instructions:

Recipe Notes:

Family Holiday Traditions:

Memories to Share:

Notes and Keepsakes:

Recipe:

Ingredients List:
_____

_____

_____

_____

_____

_____

_____

_____

Prep Time:
_____

Cooking time:
_____

Serves:
_____

Rating:
★★★★★
_____

Equipment List:
_____

_____

_____

_____

_____

_____

_____

_____

Instructions:

Recipe Notes:

Family Holiday Traditions:

Memories to Share:

Notes and Keepsakes:

Recipe:

Ingredients List:

Prep Time:

Cooking time:

Serves:

Rating: ★★★★★

Equipment List:

Instructions:

_____

_____

_____

_____

_____

_____

_____

_____

_____

_____

_____

_____

_____

_____

Recipe Notes:

_____

_____

_____

Family Holiday Traditions:

_____

_____

_____

_____

_____

_____

_____

Memories to Share:

_____

_____

_____

_____

_____

_____

_____

_____

Petal Publishing
Co.

CPSIA information can be obtained
at www.ICGtesting.com
Printed in the USA
BVHW011933021221
623109BV00003B/26

To:

Love From:

No part of this book may be scanned, reproduced or distributed in any printed or electronic form without the prior permission of the author or publisher.

Measurement Conversion Chart

Imperial	Metric	Cups 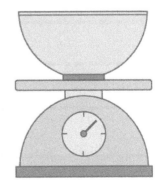
1/2 Fl.oz	15ml	1 Tablespoon
1 Fl.oz	30ml	1/8 Cup
2 Fl.oz	60 ml	1/4 Cup
4 Fl.oz	125ml	1/2 Cup
5 Fl.oz (1/4 pint)	150ml	2/3 Cup
6 Fl.oz	175 ml	3/4 Cup
8 Fl.oz	250 ml	1 Cup
12 Fl.oz	375 ml	1.1/2 Cup
16 Fl.oz	500 ml	2 Cups

Tablespoon	Teaspoon
1	3
2	6
4	12
6	18
8	24
10	30
12	36

Recipe:

Ingredients List:

Prep Time:

Cooking time:

Serves:

Rating:
★★★★★

Equipment List:

Instructions:

Recipe Notes:

Family Holiday Traditions:

_____

_____

_____

_____

_____

_____

Memories to Share:

_____

_____

_____

_____

_____

_____

_____

_____

Notes and Keepsakes:

Recipe:

Ingredients List:

Prep Time:

Cooking time:

Serves:

Rating:
★★★★★

Equipment List:

Instructions:

_____
_____
_____
_____
_____
_____
_____
_____
_____
_____
_____
_____

Recipe Notes:

_____
_____
_____
_____

Family Holiday Traditions:

_____

_____

_____

_____

_____

_____

_____

Memories to Share:

_____

_____

_____

_____

_____

_____

_____

_____

_____

Notes and Keepsakes:

Recipe:

Ingredients List:

Prep Time:

Cooking time:

Serves:

Rating: ★★★★★

Equipment List:

Instructions:

Recipe Notes:

Family Holiday Traditions:

_____

_____

_____

_____

_____

_____

_____

Memories to Share:

_____

_____

_____

_____

_____

_____

_____

_____

_____

Recipe:

Ingredients List:

Prep Time:

Cooking time:

Serves:

Rating: ★★★★★

Equipment List:

Instructions:

_____
_____
_____
_____
_____
_____
_____
_____
_____
_____
_____
_____
_____
_____

Recipe Notes:

_____
_____
_____

Family Holiday Traditions:

Memories to Share:

Recipe:

Ingredients List:

_____

_____

_____

_____

_____

_____

_____

Prep Time:

_____

Cooking time:

_____

Serves:

_____

Rating:
★★★★★

_____

Equipment List:

_____

_____

_____

_____

_____

_____

Instructions:

Recipe Notes:

Family Holiday Traditions:

_____

_____

_____

_____

_____

_____

_____

Memories to Share:

_____

_____

_____

_____

_____

_____

_____

_____

Recipe:

Ingredients List:

_____

_____

_____

_____

_____

_____

Prep Time:

_____

Cooking time:

_____

Serves:

_____

Rating:

★★★★★

Equipment List:

_____

_____

_____

_____

_____

_____

Instructions:

_____

_____

_____

_____

_____

_____

_____

_____

_____

_____

_____

_____

_____

Recipe Notes:

_____

_____

_____

_____

Family Holiday Traditions:

Memories to Share:

Notes and Keepsakes:

Recipe:

Ingredients List:

_____

_____

_____

_____

_____

_____

Prep Time:

_____

Cooking time:

_____

Serves:

_____

Rating:

★★★★★

_____

Equipment List:

_____

_____

_____

_____

_____

_____

_____

_____

Instructions:

Recipe Notes:

Family Holiday Traditions:

Memories to Share:

Notes and Keepsakes:

Recipe:

Ingredients List:

_____

_____

_____

_____

_____

_____

Prep Time:

_____

Cooking time:

_____

Serves:

_____

Rating:

★★★★★

_____

Equipment List:

_____

_____

_____

_____

_____

_____

Instructions:

Recipe Notes:

Family Holiday Traditions:

_____

_____

_____

_____

_____

_____

_____

Memories to Share:

_____

_____

_____

_____

_____

_____

_____

Notes and Keepsakes:

Recipe:

Ingredients List:
_____

_____

_____

_____

_____

_____

_____

Prep Time:
_____

Cooking time:
_____

Serves:
_____

Rating:
★★★★★

Equipment List:
_____

_____

_____

_____

_____

_____

_____

Instructions:

Recipe Notes:

Family Holiday Traditions:

_____

_____

_____

_____

_____

_____

_____

Memories to Share:

_____

_____

_____

_____

_____

_____

_____

Notes and Keepsakes:

Recipe:

Ingredients List:

_____

_____

_____

_____

_____

_____

_____

Prep Time:

_____

Cooking time:

_____

Serves:

_____

Rating:

★★★★★

_____

Equipment List:

_____

_____

_____

_____

_____

_____

_____

Instructions:

_____

_____

_____

_____

_____

_____

_____

_____

_____

_____

_____

_____

Recipe Notes:

_____

_____

_____

_____

Family Holiday Traditions:

Memories to Share:

Notes and Keepsakes:

Recipe:

Ingredients List:

_____

_____

_____

_____

_____

_____

_____

Prep Time:

_____

Cooking time:

_____

Serves:

_____

Rating:

★★★★★

_____

Equipment List:

_____

_____

_____

_____

_____

_____

Instructions:

Recipe Notes:

Family Holiday Traditions:

Memories to Share:

Notes and Keepsakes:

Recipe:

Ingredients List:
_____
_____
_____
_____
_____
_____

Prep Time:
_____

Cooking time:
_____

Serves:
_____

Rating:
★★★★★
_____

Equipment List:
_____
_____
_____
_____
_____
_____

Instructions:

Recipe Notes:

Family Holiday Traditions:

Memories to Share:

Notes and Keepsakes:

Recipe:

Ingredients List:

_____

_____

_____

_____

_____

_____

_____

Prep Time:

_____

Cooking time:

_____

Serves:

_____

Rating:

★★★★★

_____

Equipment List:

_____

_____

_____

_____

_____

_____

_____

Instructions:

_____

_____

_____

_____

_____

_____

_____

_____

_____

_____

_____

_____

_____

Recipe Notes:

_____

_____

_____

_____

Family Holiday Traditions:

_____

_____

_____

_____

_____

_____

_____

Memories to Share:

_____

_____

_____

_____

_____

_____

_____

_____

Notes and Keepsakes:

Recipe:

Ingredients List:

_____

_____

_____

_____

_____

_____

_____

_____

Prep Time:

_____

Cooking time:

_____

Serves:

_____

Rating:

★★★★★

_____

Equipment List:

_____

_____

_____

_____

_____

_____

Instructions:

Recipe Notes:

Family Holiday Traditions:

_____

_____

_____

_____

_____

_____

Memories to Share:

_____

_____

_____

_____

_____

_____

_____

_____

Notes and Keepsakes:

Recipe:

Ingredients List:

_____

_____

_____

_____

_____

_____

Prep Time:
_____

Cooking time:
_____

Serves:
_____

Rating:
★★★★★
_____

Equipment List:

_____

_____

_____

_____

_____

_____

_____

Instructions:

Recipe Notes:

Family Holiday Traditions:

Memories to Share:

Notes and Keepsakes:

Recipe:

Ingredients List:

_____

_____

_____

_____

_____

Prep Time:
_____

Cooking time:
_____

Serves:
_____

Rating:
★★★★★

Equipment List:

_____

_____

_____

_____

_____

_____

_____

Instructions:

_____

_____

_____

_____

_____

_____

_____

_____

_____

_____

_____

_____

Recipe Notes:

_____

_____

_____

_____

Family Holiday Traditions:

Memories to Share:

Notes and Keepsakes:

Recipe:

Ingredients List:

Prep Time:

Cooking time:

Serves:

Rating: ★★★★★

Equipment List:

Instructions:

Recipe Notes:

Family Holiday Traditions:

_____

_____

_____

_____

_____

_____

Memories to Share:

_____

_____

_____

_____

_____

_____

_____

Notes and Keepsakes:

Recipe:

Ingredients List:
_____
_____
_____
_____
_____
_____
_____

Prep Time:
_____

Cooking time:
_____

Serves:
_____

Rating:
★★★★★

Equipment List:
_____
_____
_____
_____
_____
_____
_____

Instructions:

Recipe Notes:

Family Holiday Traditions:

_____

_____

_____

_____

_____

_____

_____

Memories to Share:

_____

_____

_____

_____

_____

_____

_____

_____

9 781922 515728